Unicorn Press

copyright ©. all right reserved.

Test Your Color Here

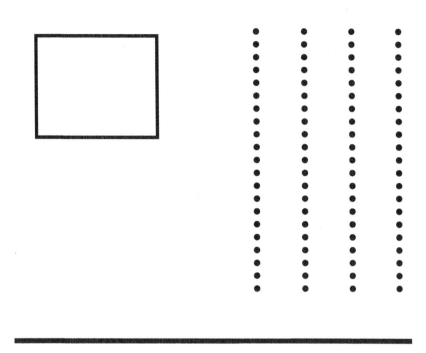

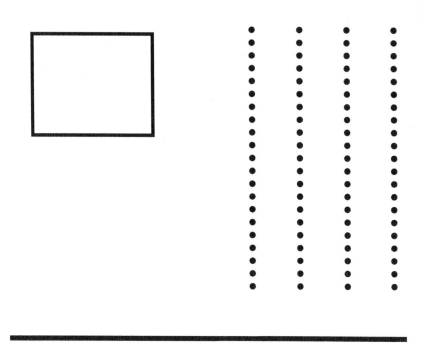

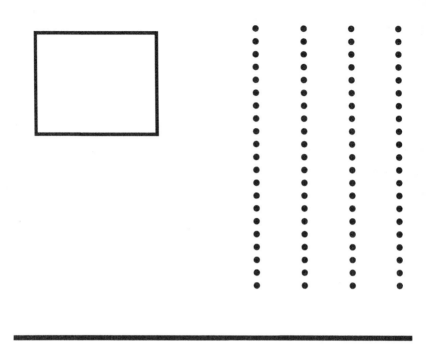

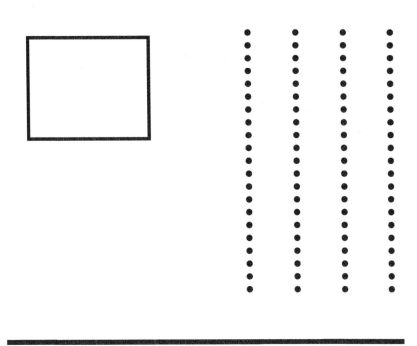

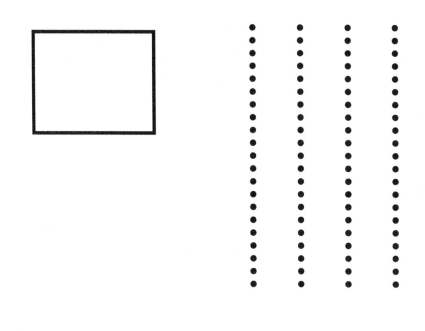

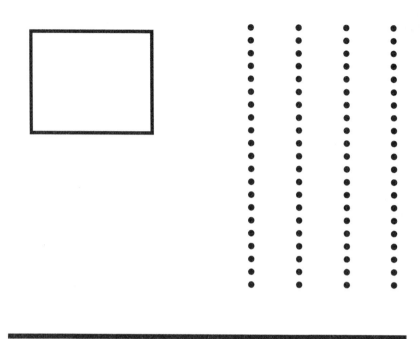

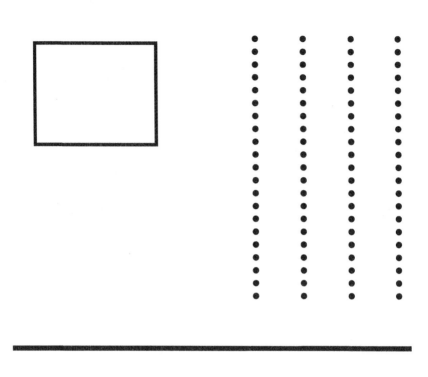

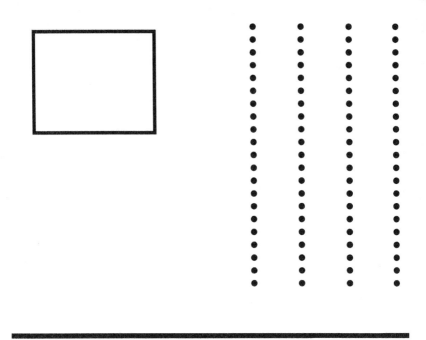

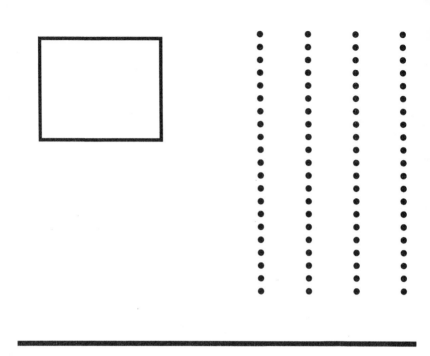

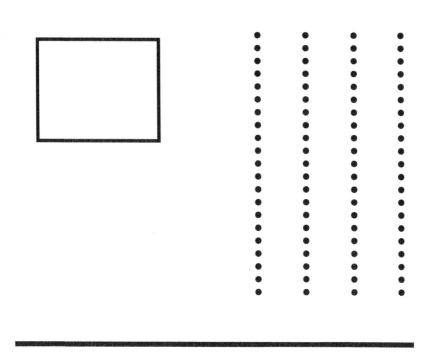

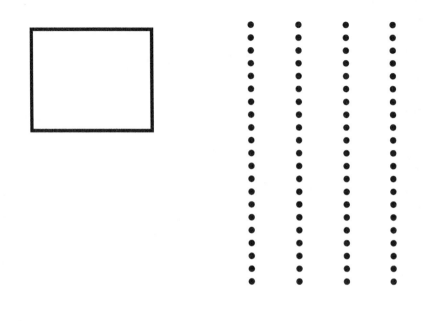

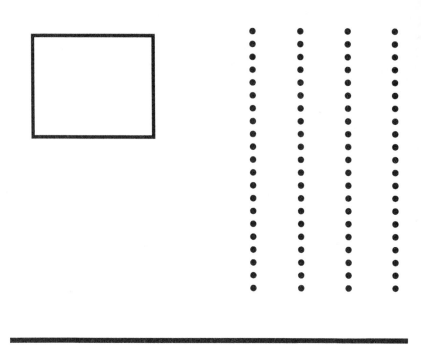

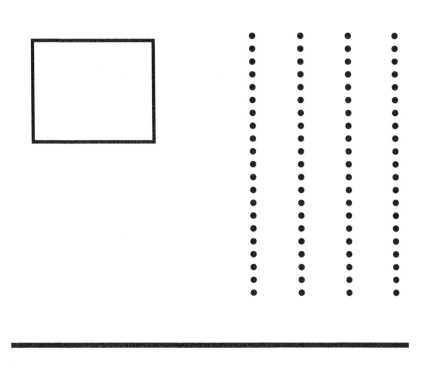

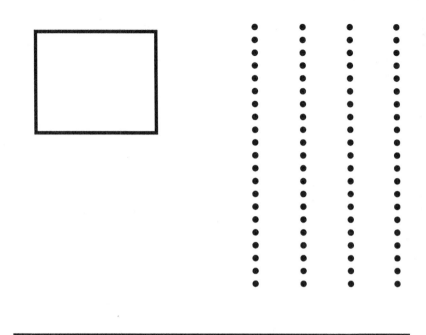

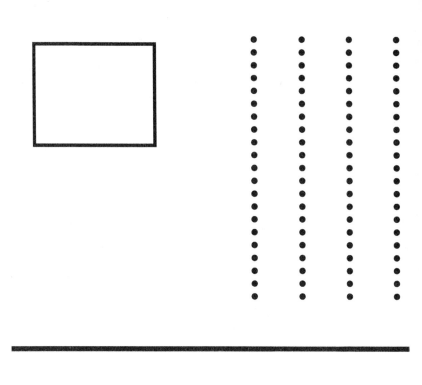

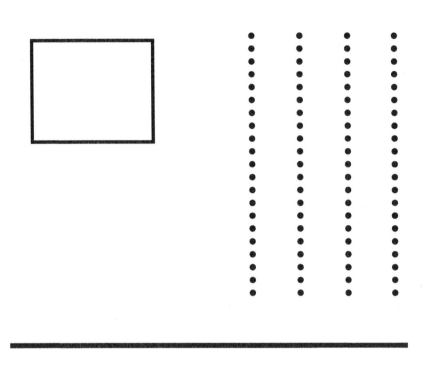

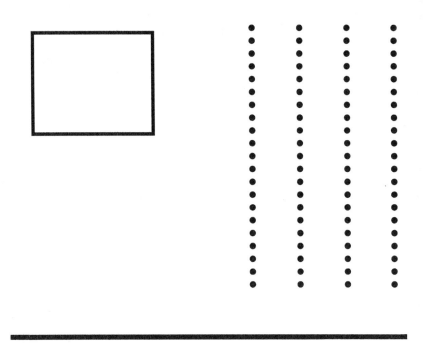

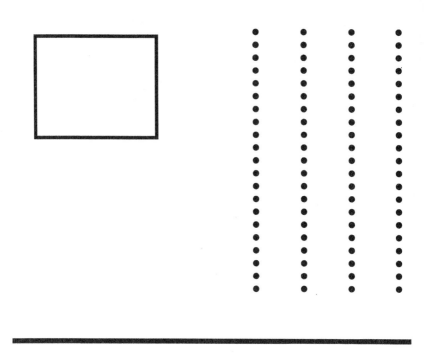

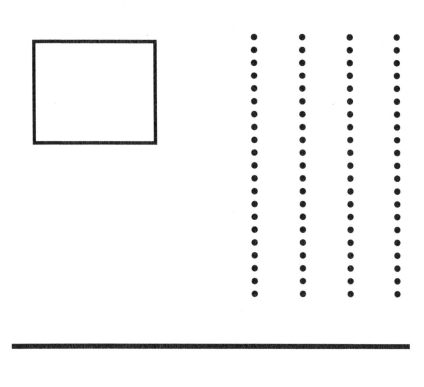

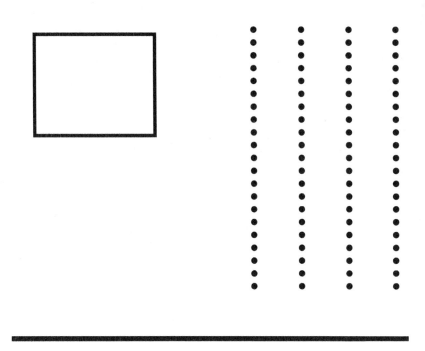

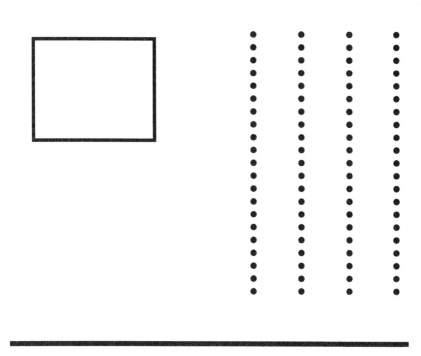

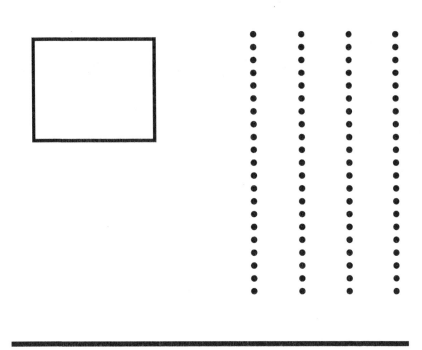

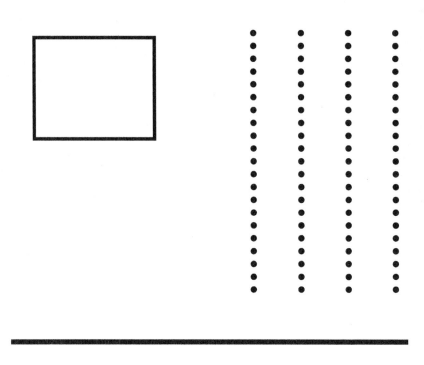

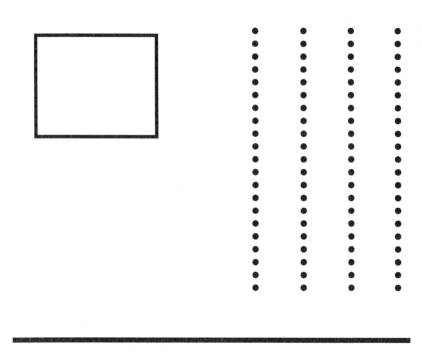

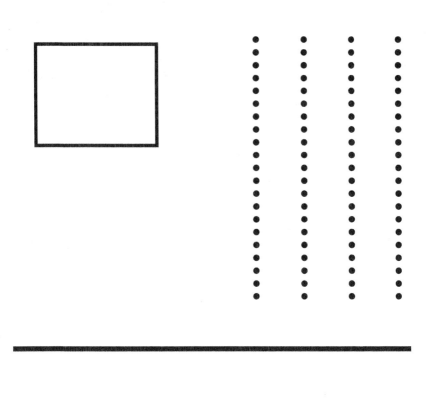

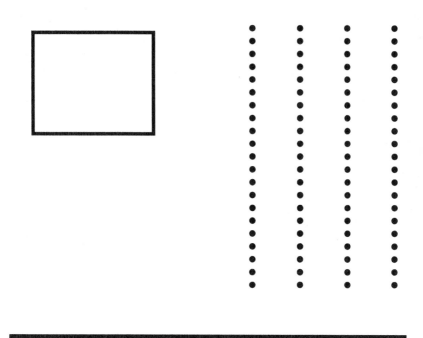

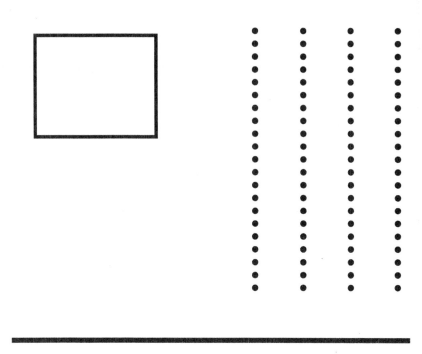

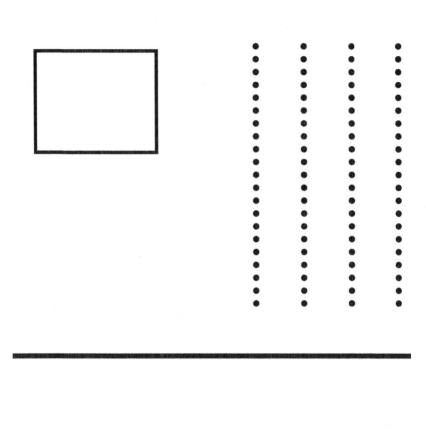

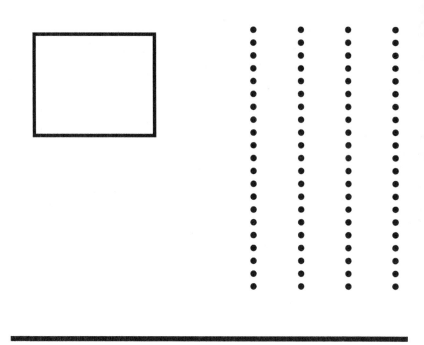

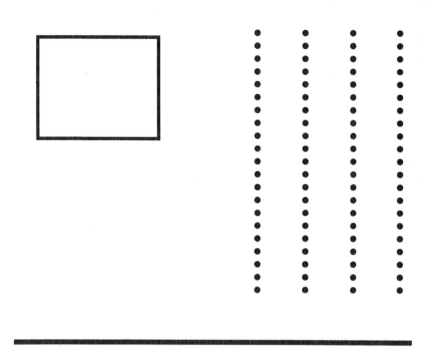

Thank You!

From Author

I Hope That Time While Coloring Was Great!

Please Rate This Book on Amazon if U Enjoyed.

UniCorn Press